Why Horses Do That

© 2003 Willow Creek Press
Illustrations © Beth Messina

Published by Willow Creek Press, P.O. Box 147, Minocqua, Wisconsin 54548

Edited by Andrea Donner

Library of Congress Cataloging-in-Publication Data
Dines, Lisa, 1955-
Why horses do that : a collection of curious equine behavior / Lisa Dines ;
illustrations by Beth Messina.
p. cm.
ISBN 1-57223-707-4 (hardcover : alk. paper)
1. Horses--Behavior--Miscellanea. I. Title.
SF281.D56 2003
636.1--dc21
2003011410

Printed in Canada

Why Horses Do That

A Collection of Curious Equine Behaviors

Text by Lisa Dines

Illustrated by Beth Messina

Willow Creek® PRESS

MINOCQUA, WISCONSIN

Acknowledgement

Thanks to my husband, Joe, for his guidance and creative input and to my son, Dustin, for his technical advice and hardware support. Without my beautiful nieces, many drawings would not have been possible. Thank you Brea, Nicki, Amanda, Keni, Miranda, Kaeleigh, and Analeise. And thank you Kim, for donating your time and gorgeous horse, Solomon, to this interesting project. Lastly, I am most appreciative of my mare, Dottie, whose wonderful acting talent made several of my illustrations come to life.

— B.M.

I would like to dedicate this book to all of us who care for horses — whether rideable or not — and to the horses for the noble and heartfelt effort they return.

— L.D.

I once heard a quote that went something like: "God didn't give man wings, so he gave us horses." I would like to dedicate this book to all the marvelous horses in my life. They have taught me so much and have given wings to my unending passion of trying to illustrate their magnificence. I am honored to be able to share them with you.

— B.M.

TABLE OF CONTENTS

PREFACE

Because the horse is one of the only domestic animals I can think of whose normal, friendly behaviors can shake you to your very core, I felt privileged when my editor asked me to explore forty of their most interesting quirks in depth.

Have you ever experienced the unexpected and unnerving "magic fingers" pulsating throughout your body when your horse neighs to its best friend while you are riding on its back? Or how about your equine buddy whose greatest desire seems to be to drop and roll in any body of water (or on a sandy beach or arena) with you still in the saddle? Why do horses act this way?

You also might not know that horses are intestinally-challenged, with certain grasses causing aller-gies and other plants being toxic to them. Or that horses get ulcers, sleep standing up, eat dirt, and drink out of muddy rain puddles.

I thought I knew everything there was to know about the goofy-looking flehmen response with that upraised lip, or why my horse misbehaved for me but not for my trainer. Easy, I thought, "He's just being a horse" or "he felt like it." But when I dug a little deeper, I discovered there were many quirky horse behaviors that I knew noth-ing about.

From horse behavior such as rearing, bucking, biting, squealing, and kicking, to horse stubbornness in refusing to go, to whoa, to load, and to unload, along with the basic physical uniqueness of the equine eyes, backs, legs, and stomachs, I've tried to explore every nuance of the wonderful, lovable horse.

I hope you enjoy reading these fascinating facts as much as I've enjoyed researching them. And perhaps this little book will help you to understand your horse a little better, and pause to wonder why he's acting so strange, or so funny, or so completely endearing. Hand it to the horse for bringing so many of us together in common enjoyment and understanding!

Why do horses kick if approached from the rear?

Horses have nearly 360 degrees of panoramic vision on each side of their bodies from the large eyes placed on the sides of their heads; however, there are two major areas where horses have blind spots. The first is directly in front of and under their noses (where they have long, sensitive whiskers to help them feel what's there), and the other is directly in back of their tails, where nature has provided them with powerful kicking and running devices — their hind legs and pelvic structure.

When you approach a horse from the rear, he can't see or smell you and he may kick out in surprise at an unidentified noise or touch. From the horse's perspective, you could be a predator or another horse coming to steal his food or water.

You must talk to a horse to let him know you are a friendly human when approaching from the rear. If you know a horse well enough, you can even put your hand on his rump to let him know you are there.

If a horse kicks, bites at, or strikes deliberately at a person they can see, that horse must be re-trained so it no longer perceives humans as threats or competition. The good news is that even severely-abused horses can forgive and learn to trust again with specialized retraining.

WHY DO HORSES PACE, CRIB, CHEW WOOD, AND BITE THEMSELVES?

Horses are designed to spend their waking hours in the simple and necessary equine pleasures of eating, moving, and grooming — in that order. When kept in isolation with no grazing or exercise for long periods of time, horses simply get stressed. Many horses find relief by engaging in artificial, vigorous forms of eating, moving, and grooming, such as "weaving" from side to side in their stalls, rapidly pacing the inside of the stall or along a fence-line, taking hold of a hard surface with their teeth, arching their necks and sucking in air, called "cribbing," chewing and eating wooden surfaces, or biting themselves repeatedly. These activities stimulate brain chemicals such as endorphins and dopamine, which produce contentment and block pain.

Excess caloric intake can also be a contributing problem to stress. Horses are designed to eat plain, fibrous grasses one mouthful at a time continuously throughout the day, not several pounds of sweetened, high-fat, high-protein grain concentrates only once or twice a day. When overfed and inactive, a toxic overload is produced in horses' bodies that can seriously damage their internal organs, hooves, and moods.

Without exercise and a proper diet, horses can develop colic, founder, ulcers, abnormally worn-down teeth and hooves, or behavioral problems like aggression.

WHY DO HORSES "SPOOK" AT THINGS?

Say you are riding along a forest path and there is a cut log next to the trail. It doesn't move, so your horse may not have noticed it from the side, but as you ride past, the concentric rings and dark core in the middle (which could resemble a giant eyeball if you're a horse) come suddenly into the right position under the sharp-focus area of your horse's eye, and your horse may jump as if he had never seen a log before! To understand this, you have to know how a horse sees, smells, hears, and thinks about the world, which is quite different than a human's experience.

Horses can hear, smell, and see a far greater number of movements than we can. In the wild, their lives depend on it. However, as prey animals, their eyes are placed on the sides of their heads, which may allow them to see nearly 360 degrees, but causes greater limitations when it comes to depth perception, close-up focus, and binocular vision.

Unless a horse can move its head and place an object directly in front of its face so it can view it with both eyes, or touch or smell the object with its nose, it's hard for a horse to accurately determine how near or far, deep or shallow, or dangerous or benign an object is. In addition, horses' eyes cannot focus as well on close-up details. They need to move their heads up and down to place the object underneath an area in their eye that focuses close up, whereas humans' eyes automatically adjust as objects move closer. We truly must rely on an amazing bond of trust with our horses when riding to overcome all these differences.

WHY DO HORSES DRINK OUT OF MUDDY PUDDLES?

You would think that a horse would prefer drinking out of a clean water trough rather than out of a muddy puddle if it had the choice, but you might be wrong. After a rain, horses seem to enjoy the taste of the fresh water that accumulates in shallow puddles better than the large amount of "stale" H_2O sitting in their regular troughs. In the wild, horses create their own mudholes by pawing at the ground surrounding natural springs, then drinking from this. The pawing stirs up minerals the horses seek in their diet, which they drink along with the water. Similarly, horses drinking from streams and lakes usually paw the water first before drinking. Sometimes this has the effect of clearing debris or floating plant matter off the surface, but if the water source has a sandy bottom, this can create an excess amount of sand ingested with the water, which can accumulate in the horses' intestines and create a blockage called an impaction.

While horses do prefer fresh water, you may notice that if you are traveling and ask your horse to drink fresh water that is from a different source than that which they are accustomed to, they may refuse to drink at all. Since it is essential that a horse drinks water to maintain performance and health in hot weather, after exercise, for proper digestion, and while traveling, you can put a sweet-tasting drink mix into a new water source to get your horse to drink. Because the horse's health depends on continually

flushing the sand and plant matter from the intestine to keep it clear from blockage, water, no matter what the source, is essential.

Drinking out of rain puddles also simulates the full neck extension of watering from a lake or stream, which is probably more comfortable and natural for a horse than drinking from a trough with a neck in a more upraised position. In addition, a horse may be just too lazy to walk all the way to his regular water trough when there is a perfectly good mud puddle on the ground right next to him!

WHY DO HORSES EAT POISONOUS PLANTS AND DIE?

Horses evolved eating native grasses and plants, not the exotic, decorative, tropical and flowering plants that humans like to plant around their homes. Pruned clippings or hedges of oleander, rhododendron, laurel, jasmine, hydrangea, Japanese yew, and other plants are toxic to horses, and have unfortunately been given to horses or placed within reach of horses who suffer quick, violent deaths if they eat them.

Star thistle, tarweed, hound's tongue, locoweed, vetch, sorghum, buttercup, foxglove, monkshood, some lupines (Texas bluebonnet is low in toxicity,) and other common weed species will poison horses slowly over time, and can still be harmful when baled with good hay that is aged and dry. Poisonous fungus and ergot molds occurring on some grasses and clovers can also be very deadly to horses. Only one mouthful of water hemlock — whose enticing, tender shoots in the spring come up in boggy areas throughout North America — is sufficient to kill a horse in minutes.

Horses usually avoid toxic plants because of the bitter taste and bad smell — unless there is nothing else to eat. Horses do best grazing day and night (on at least one acre per equine) on a diet of safe grasses with a constant supply of clean water.

WHY DO HORSES WANT TO PAW AND ROLL WHEN CROSSING A CREEK?

Because they're hot, sweaty, uncomfortable, or itchy! The urge to "stop, drop and roll" takes place for several reasons — mostly because horses have extremely sensitive skin that is exposed to insects, the elements, sweaty saddle blankets, and badly-fitting tack. Horses can't really scratch or massage their own spines in any other way. Whether a horse rolls in dirt, mud, water, or stall shavings (which is why stalls need to be built large enough for rolling) rolling is said to be a horsey equivalent of going to a chiropractor for a spinal adjustment (especially if a horse rolls all the way over and back again.)

Hot, sweaty horses are almost impossible to convince not to paw and roll when wading through water during a ride. The secret is to allow them to lower their heads and drink if they are thirsty, but to pull their heads up and urge them forward if they paw and splash. And of course, horses enjoy a bath from a hose to cool off in the summertime, too.

WHY DO HORSES BREATHE INTO EACH OTHER'S NOSTRILS?

When two horses meet for the first time (or after a separation) they will exchange exhalations through their nostrils. Horses are saying "hello" in this way, and will remember the smell of each other's breath like we recall someone's name. After a few initial breaths, the intensity of the "huffing" can then escalate or decrease depending upon the information exchanged. Increased, harder breathing between horses indicates a desire to work out dominance issues, and can lead to biting, squealing, striking or turning around to pummel with hard kicks from hind legs. (This is why it may not be a good idea to allow horses to exchange breaths while riding them!) Horses who have already established herd rank may exchange a few familiar puffs, then proceed to mutual grooming, grazing, or standing contentedly next to one another.

WHY DO HORSES FIGHT, BUT REFUSE TO LEAVE ONE ANOTHER?

Cohesive, peaceful herd behavior can only be achieved after horses fight to establish a pecking order. Horses gain security (and nourishment) from having an established rank order for eating, drinking, and interacting socially.

When humans ask horses to "hit the trail" (or arena) for riding, horses can feel quite alone without their equine companions who give order to their lives. Fortunately, humans can and do fulfill the need horses have for a more dominant being to tell them when they should move, stop, eat, and drink — which is probably why we have been successful at managing them for so long. A horse that is "herd bound" or "barn sour" and refuses to leave an area where other horses congregate is merely afraid and can be trained to overcome this with the right handling.

Why do horses behave better with the trainer than they do with you?

It is so frustrating to watch your horse fail to exhibit those troublesome or dangerous behaviors he does with you when the trainer rides him. It is useless to blame your horse or yourself for this. A horse is simply reacting (in most cases) to how and when a request to do something is given, and to how and when they are rewarded for the "right answer." A sensitive, experienced trainer has developed better "feel" for horse behavior over the years he or she has been riding and studying hundreds of horses (or else you would be the trainer and riders would be calling you!). A good trainer is also not as afraid of your horse as you may be, and is not as apt to take personally a horse's misbehavior the way an owner can (two things we can subconsciously transmit to our horses when we ride.)

You have several options should your skill, desire, or patience level fall short of what your horse needs. You can have someone else train your horse; you can sell that horse and buy another with more training; or you can take lessons from your trainer on that horse and expand both you and your horse's horizons simultaneously. Remember, the more confident and relaxed you are, the more your horse will enjoy your company and direction.

Why do horses squeal and strike?

Two horses meeting for the first time always need to work out dominance issues. A horse of either gender who is clearly communicating they intend to stand and fight rather than run away, will sometimes squeal and strike.

When horses first meet, they usually sniff each other's nostrils in order to recognize each other and establish rank. After breath is exchanged, one horse may give a little bite to the other's jaw, and the first may counter with a squeal and a strike (with a raised forefoot) as if to say "No!" or "Forget it!"

Male horses also sometimes need find out whether a mare is sexually receptive. A mare who is not in season will sometimes squeal and strike at a stallion to communicate that she does is not ready for his advances. Stallions will also strike and squeal when meeting and fighting over mares.

WHY DO BABY HORSES "CLACK" THEIR TEETH?

Foals and younger horses display a submissive behavior toward more dominant horses by lowering their neck and head, opening their mouth, and "clacking" or clapping their teeth together repeatedly. With this behavior, they are clearly communicating their subordinate position. They are basically begging for mercy, and the tactic seems to quickly diffuse any further aggression towards them.

Clacking may be related to actions of grooming another horse, or may simply be a posture of appeasement common to horses and other equids. (Teeth clacking is also displayed by submissive female donkeys during mating.) Since the young horses mainly direct teeth clacking toward the mouths of other horses, it seems to resemble the mouth-licking appeasement gesture of a young or submissive dog towards another dog, or the action of a baby bird begging for food from a parent's mouth.

Some horses three or four-years-old will still clack their teeth when meeting a strange horse for the first time or if they are trying to indicate clearly their desire to be submissive. This action can look a bit silly when the "teeth clacker" is taller and older than its "threatening" friend!

While it is usually effective to be submissive within a herd at a younger age, clacking teeth is completely futile when a family group of wild horses decides its time to drive a young offspring out at sexual maturity.

WHY DO HORSES RAISE THEIR UPPER LIPS IN A "HORSE LAUGH"?

A horse displaying the facial expression of a curled upper lip pressed back on the nose, with its neck and head extended upward, is exhibiting the "flehmen" response. A horse does this when it detects an odor worthy of pressing into a sensitive olfactory discrimination area called the vomeronasal organ, which is located in its nasal cavity. The flehmen response increases the flow of air through the nostrils, bringing the scent through openings behind the incisors on the upper palette to the vomeronasal organ.

Reptiles bring scents into their mouths on their tongues, but horses, goats, cats, and other mammals (except higher primates and humans) can be seen performing the same response with a wrinkled top lip and an open mouth.

Perfumes and lotions on human hands can cause horses to curl their lips up, and a stallion will make this face when he examines a mare's urine to detect if she is in heat. The vomeronasal organ is orientated with the brain's sexual behavior center, and is used to decipher the pheromones a mare emits.

Of course, this funny facial expression makes a horse look as if he were laughing (and we can never be totally sure they aren't)!

WHY DO HORSES SOMETIMES TRY TO BITE EACH OTHER'S KNEES?

When horses fight or play fight, they will go for each other's knees in an attempt to bring one horse to the ground in a kneeling position so they are unable to fight or flee. (The kneeling horse is the loser of that round!) Horses will protect their vulnerable legs from being bitten by dodging, backing up, rearing, or blocking the attacker's jaw with their heads. Stallions have been seen disciplining young males who challenge them by quickly biting first the knees, then the hocks and thighs to make them completely lie down with their legs folded underneath them. This establishes undisputed dominance since the youngster is rendered completely helpless on the ground.

Why do horses rear?

A rearing horse communicates a desire to stand ground rather than flee. Rearing is done to gain height, inflict damage by striking another horse's face and body with the forelegs, and to bring the force of a horse's weight down on another's back during play or serious fighting.

Horses that rear under saddle are hopefully only doing this on cue as a well-controlled, impressive trick! Rearing was once employed by warhorse trainers for use during battle, and is nowadays taught to police horses for crowd control.

If a horse rears for any other reason under saddle, it is usually because that horse feels unable or unwilling to move forward or backward, and goes straight up instead. This can certainly be a problem for a horse and rider. One commonly-suggested but senseless remedy is to pull the horse over backwards, which could of course injure or kill both horse and rider.

A horse in the initial stages of saddle training should be kept moving forward quietly and steadily, and be thoroughly desensitized to overcome its fears of objects on or around its body to prevent such reactions as rearing or bucking. Specialized retraining is needed when a horse deliberately rears to remove a rider.

WHY DO HORSES BUCK?

The best reason for a horse to buck or "kick up its heels" is to express health, fitness and pleasure of motion without a rider. Horses running or playing will often buck and leap just for the fun of it. (Cold, windy weather seems to encourage this lively movement in horses.)

The downside of bucking is when it is done by a terrified horse with something on its back or around its belly, which it feels needs to be removed. This type of horse bucks and grunts as if there were a mountain lion gripping its body with sharp claws. Since wild horses are successful at dislodging predators from their bodies by vigorous bucking, this can be a lifesaver, but bucking under saddle usually indicates fear, discomfort, or pain.

Saddles and blankets need to be carefully examined before being put on a horse's back. A thorn or sticker in the horse's skin can irritate an otherwise gentle horse to the point of madness when a rider's weight drives it in even further. Likewise, a bee sting or painful insect bite can cause a bucking reaction as a horse attempts to dislodge the insect (which can, of course, also dislodge the rider). A horse's back should likewise be inspected before saddling to detect sores or painful lumps.

The bareback and saddle "broncs" seen in rodeo shows are trying to rid themselves of a bucking strap that is placed uncomfortably around their flanks. Rodeo bucking horses may originally have had a frightening experience during saddle training, which instead of being resolved was encouraged for the sport.

WHY DO HORSES HATE RIDING IN TRAILERS?

Imagine going on a trip of an unknown duration and destination in a noisy, dusty, bouncing, swerving, dark box while trying to remain standing up. Sound like fun? Take a ride down a busy highway in your horse trailer (without the horse) to experience how your horse feels!

Horses are naturally programmed for forward movement, and can feel claustrophobic in a small space they can only back out of, trapped between a "butt chain" and a feed box. They may even get carsick!

In order to get a horse to love to travel, you must make it a pleasant experience. (Not so different than making sure children have snacks and mental stimulation during a long road trip.)

If you feed sweetened grain to a horse in a trailer, they will build up excess energy that has no outlet. Instead, give a horse hay to munch on to keep it calm and occupied during the ride. Also, a trailer with windows or slats that enable a horse to see is better than one with no eye holes. A mesh fly mask will protect their eyes from debris and dust. Additionally, driving slowly around curves minimizes any "crack the whip" sensation your horse might feel on his end of your rig. If you do all of these things for your horse, he can learn to love trailering.

Why are horses so hard to load in trailers?

It is normal behavior for a flight animal to fear entering a small, dark, dead-end box, and to hear a door shut behind them. While it is their natural instinct not to enter the trailer, there are ways you can help your horse overcome his fear of loading.

If you load your horse into the trailer and then immediately unload him, and then repeat this action multiple times, your horse will eventually feel confident that one action will follow the other. If your trailer has a "drop ramp," practice leading your horse calmly across a piece of plywood on the ground before asking him to climb the wooden trailer ramp. Back your horse out of a narrow stall before backing him out of a narrow trailer. Train your horse to listen and trust your voice commands such as "easy," "back," "step down," and train your horse to enter a trailer on a command from behind. Slant-load trailers (where horses stand tied side by side) may be less restrictive than front-loaders because horses can be turned around and led out.

Never scare a horse into a trailer. A horse will enter when he feels comfortable, and after he has had a rewarding experience for doing so. Make sure you leave plenty of time *before* an important event for trailer training so there is no pressure.

WHY DO HORSES DIE FROM SERIOUS STOMACHACHES?

Horses are physically incapable of vomiting, and if overfed or after eating something toxic, they must wait a long (and sometimes painful) time for their digestion and elimination system to fix the problem. "Colic" is the word for a stomachache in equines. Horses can build up excess gas from eating rich feed, or have an allergic reaction to

feed that can cause pain. When a horse is "colicking," or experiencing severe stomach pain, they will roll repeatedly without shaking the dirt off when they rise, sweat, pace, turn and look at and bite at their flanks, and refuse feed and water. When gas builds up because an impaction or a twisted section is blocking an intestine, the intestine can rupture and the horse will die.

Knowing what and how much to feed a horse is crucial for the horse owner. For example, if a horse is fed on the ground and picks up too much sand with its feed, the sand can cause an impaction. If a horse does not drink plenty of water with its feed, the dry matter can become impacted (which sometimes happens in the winter when a water supply is iced over). Eating too much of a toxic plant can cause stomach pain, or even the horse's death.

Horses also get ulcers if they have empty stomachs for most of the day, especially if they are nervous or have less efficient digestion due to old age. The pain of an ulcer can cause a horse to colic and refuse to eat, which only compounds the problem. Older horses should be on pasture twenty-four hours a day. You can maintain a horse on antacids or special medication if they are ulcer-prone, but generally speaking, a horse grazing on pasture with a supply of clean drinking water will have the fewest stomachaches.

WHY DO HORSES "NICKER" WHEN YOU FEED THEM?

That "*uh huh huh*" sound that domesticated horses make when they see you coming (hopefully with food) is oh-so-heartwarming and cheerful! This low, vibrating sound is also shared between mares and their foals, and stallions and mares before mating. It is a greeting of deep affection, but it is not always connected to feeding.

Horses rely on sounds, smells, and body language to communicate their intentions to one another, and to trusted human friends as well. Horses make five main types of sounds: a squeal, a nicker, a neigh or whinny, a blow or snort, and a seldom-heard scream that occurs between rival stallions.

Why do horses whinny or neigh?

The whinny or neigh, while not as high-pitched as a squeal or scream, is still loud enough to carry over long distances. It varies in pitch, starting high and dropping to half the starting frequency. The whinny is used to maintain contact between herd members when they are separated or out of each other's sight. Horses as far as a quarter of a mile away can hear another horse whinny. When wild horses wish to announce their presence to another wild band, they call out a warning whinny.

A whinny can take the place of a nicker if a horse is especially enthusiastic about receiving food. Horses recognize and respond to whinnies from their own herd members as a form of identification.

Why do horses blow and snort?

The "blow" is a short, intense pop of air out of a horse's nostrils, almost like a goose's honk. There is no mistaking a wild stallion's loud blow as an alarm call to his band. The rest of the herd comes instantly to attention — heads up and ready to run. A blow out of the nose may also serve to quickly clear any obstruction to better smell and identify approaching danger.

The snort is a softer version of the blow, which, while still indicating alarm, does not necessarily serve to communicate that alarm to any other horses. There are several versions of the snort — from the quickest, done only once or twice, to a deep, rolling, drawn-out affair that sounds very ominous indeed. A horse that is intensely frightened of an object or person may use a rolling snort while they stand their ground, wary and staring.

Both snorting and blowing may be attempts to try to warn away approaching danger, similar to the warning bark or growl of a dog, but horses quickly turn into flight animals if the warning doesn't work!

WHY DO HORSES COME IN SO MANY DIFFERENT COLORS?

Millions of years ago when the first horse, Eohippus, hid in the bushes like a tiny deer, it could very well have been colored like one too. Before Equus Caballus, the "modern horse," evolved during the

Pleistocene epoch and humans began painting pictures of the animals around them, we can only guess at the color of early horses.

Cave paintings in Europe show wild horses with dun coloration: yellowish or reddish-brown bodies, upright black manes, black tails and lower legs, with stripes on ear rims, backs, and legs. Dun was not the only color, however. From remains found and characteristics continued in horses descended from them, the diminutive Tundra horse of Siberia was white, and the large forest horse of Europe was probably dapple grey. Recently, carcasses of a subspecies of modern horse, *Equus Lambei*, were found well preserved after being frozen in glacial ice in the Yukon Territory of Canada. This 44-inch-tall horse had reddish body hair, yellowish-brown lower legs, and a long, flowing blond mane and tail.

Natural selection favors "earth tones" on prey animals so they blend well with the surrounding environment (or stripes to dazzle and confuse the eye of a predator when moving in a large herd, such as those found on zebras). When people began to domesticate, feed, and offer protection to horses, "flashy," light-colored and noticeable newborn foals with lots of white survived, were prized and admired, and then selectively bred.

Human intervention in the natural colors of horses has led to the dazzling array of colors seen in today's domesticated horses, including those with blue, green, or gold eyes. If horse color were left up to Mother Nature, most horses would be bay, chestnut, brown, or black.

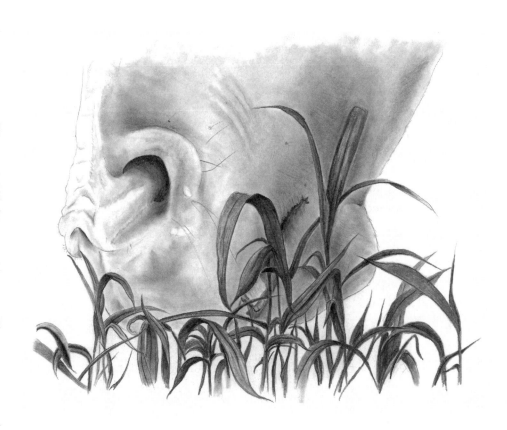

WHY DO HORSES RESEMBLE RHINOS AND TAPIRS MORE THAN THEIR DOMESTIC BUDDIES, COWS AND SHEEP?

There is a basic difference in the way horses (and rhinos and tapirs) digest food that gives them an edge for survival when not fed and protected by man. Horses do not have to rest and chew their cud to digest food the way cows and sheep do. Horses have an organ called the cecum that breaks down plant cellulose quickly, while a horse is "on the run." Also, due to their mobility and size, horses can travel further and faster to new sources of food.

Although horses are often seen sharing grassland with ruminants, the equine's ecological niche extends to the inhospitable, dry, rocky areas with low-protein plants that cannot sustain cattle and sheep. This is why wild horses (with a constant source of water) survive and reproduce so well on the high deserts and rugged terrain of half a dozen Western states today.

There is one more advantage (for the horse) of not being a cud-chewing ruminant. Because cattle, sheep, and goats can hold their food for hours longer in more digestive chambers, and extract more usable energy from a smaller amount of overall feed, they are generally raised as meat animals, while the horse is not.

WHY DO HORSES DOMESTICATE SO WELL?

The reason man domesticated the animals he did (including the horse and some species of wild ass) was because these animals were adaptable, curious, non-territorial, non-aggressive, dependent, playful, and submissive. Similar to the house sparrow, starling, pigeon, rat, mouse, and cockroach (but perhaps a bit more useful), wild horses preferred to hang out with humans and benefit from our bounty. We, in turn, understood their usefulness to us and started to put them to work and tend to their needs in exchange.

Submissiveness and curiosity are not traits found in all types of equids, however. A relative of the domestic horse, the Przewalski (pronounced *sheh-val-ski*) Horse remains in its original wild form today because they are not at all interested in getting up close and personal with humans! They act aggressively and independently towards us. Similarly, many species of the ass family — the onager, kiang, zebra, and quagga — are usually found in the wild or in zoos for the same reason.

Horses have been our essential work partners throughout the evolution of human culture, and only until recently have horses been relegated to the status of a luxury companion animal in the United States. Many horse people feel they cannot live without their horses on a daily basis, and the telepathy between our two species can be extraordinary.

Why do horses have "horse teeth"?

The jaws of the horse provide side to side, as well as up and down, motion to the twelve large molars and six incisors in an adult horse's mouth. Horses' molars are dense, tall, constantly growing, have ridges of enamel for rough grinding, and are placed at an angle for shearing. These are the teeth a large grazing herbivore needs to completely pulverize plant matter (and the sandy soil that often sticks to it) into a bacteria-friendly, digestible soup.

As horses age, they typically need dental work to make sure their teeth meet together for complete grinding. Most wild horses die from malnutrition, not disease, because they can no longer eat properly due to missing or worn down teeth.

Incisors must meet together in the front of the jaw to be effective nippers. If the horse has either an under or an overbite and is allowed to forage and graze, they will pull up plants — roots, dirt, and all — ingest too much sand and get a sand impaction in the intestines, which is often fatal. A horse with a mis-aligned bite must be fed food that is already in small pieces.

Male horses (and occasionally mares) grow pointed teeth in the spaces between the molars and inci-sors on both the top and bottom jaws, called canine teeth. Canine teeth are usually rounded off and reduced in height so as not to cause pain or injury when the horse's cheek presses against them. Some horses grow small, sharp, shallow-rooted "wolf teeth," which erupt next to the first molar on the top jaw. These are removed or they will be dislodged by the bit and cause the horse pain.

Why do horses go lame?

A horse's legs are disproportionately long and light with less muscle and thinner bones compared to the rest of its body. This gives the horse a longer stride and faster speed, but it also means the legs are more susceptible to injury by blows or concussion. Additionally, the whole weight of a horse is taken on one leg during certain gaits, leg injuries are slow to heal because the horse must distribute its weight on all four legs to stand up, and many horses are started under saddle to begin performance and show careers, including racing, at an early age (before bones and joints are fully mature). These factors all contribute to horses having such high incidences of breaks, strains, pulls, and cuts on the legs.

Hoof problems, however, are the biggest source of debilitating lameness in equines. Improper shoeing and trimming, leaving shoes on too long, overfeeding, stepping on objects, and infection all produce painful lameness that can render a horse unable to move. There is an old saying, "No foot, no horse." The good news is most hoof lameness is totally preventable.

WHY DO SOME HORSES REFUSE TO "GO"?

Who hasn't been on a trail ride, tried to get a rental horse to increase its speed past a walk, and failed? Horses become "insensitive" to the cues of riders when they are in pain, tired, afraid, bored, or when they see no reason to get very "excited" because of their age and/or temperament. Rental string horses are usually chosen in the first place because they are "bomb-proof" — easy-going, safe for all types of riders, and just doing their job if nobody falls off. Seasoned rental horses often know in what areas of the trail the wrangler in charge increases the pace, and will speed up only when the lead horse does, but not so fast as to overtake the leader.

This is proper trail horse etiquette, by the way!

There are a few other reasons horses refuse to move forward when asked. In the early stages of training, horses often have problems balancing the weight of a rider, (in addition to usually being young and relatively uncoordinated themselves), and sometimes hesitate to move forward because they are afraid they will fall down. A horse being asked to do something for the first time often needs to investigate objects first by smell, sight, and touch before proceeding. This is why it is good to practice in the same arena over the same jumps or course *before* the show, and not *during* the show, if you can!

Why do horses refuse to "whoa"?

Teaching your horse a solid "halt" or "whoa" can be a lifesaver. When driving horses learn to pull a cart or carriage, they are usually taught to absolutely freeze when they hear "whoa," and not move an inch until they are given another command such as "walk on." This is in case something goes wrong with the harness or vehicle that needs to be repaired before scaring the horse and causing an accident.

"Whoa" is a useful trick to teach a riding horse as well. When you are mounting your horse, there is nothing more irritating and unsafe than the horse that begins to walk away when you are only half on. One method of training your horse to halt for mounting is to give them a treat once you are in the saddle, but only if they remain perfectly still. (If a horse bends their neck back toward you, they cannot go forward easily anyway. Done at high speed this is the emergency "one-rein stop" used on a runaway horse under saddle.)

Horses will refuse to stop when heading home, when following a lead horse, when untrained or insensitive to cues, and when panicking. Many people who are afraid of horses have had a horse "run away with them" (back to the barn), and then try to scrape them off on a tree, fence, doorway, or side of a building! This is dangerous for both horse and rider, and requires retraining by someone more experienced. Horses become "hard-mouthed" (insensitive or resistant to rein cues) because riders jerk hard on the reins, causing them to pull brace and stiffen, or keep such constant pressure on the mouth that the horse gets confused.

Why do some horses prefer standing out in the rain to being under shelter?

In general, horses do not like enclosed spaces. Even when forced to remain in a shelter, horses would rather see what is all around them and be able to make a fast getaway unhindered by walls. The sound a metal roof can make when heavy rain, hail, tree branches, or debris (or worst-case scenario lightning) hits it can be deafening and scary, so horses may prefer to stand under large trees during storms or out in the open.

Horses have dense, warm undercoats in the winter (if they are not clipped), a layer of fat under their skin for insulation, and a longer outer coat which can have vertical swirl patterns that act as little gullies to carry rain to the ground.

Waterproof rainsheets are good for horses standing out in the rain, especially for clipped, thin, or older animals. Excess dampness can cause a bacterial infection called "rainrot." Insulated blankets protect horses from snow and cold, but it's more important to keep horses supplied with lots of hay in the winter. Hay takes the most energy to eat and digest, and as a result, keeps horses warm.

WHY DO HORSES HAVE SUCH A VARIETY OF BODY TYPES?

It is believed there were originally four basic horse types: wetland pony, wetland horse, desert pony, and desert horse. The pony types were genetically designed to be short, and could be used to downsize a breed. Horse forms were larger and could make a breed bigger. Wetland forms were stockier, hairier (including longer hair on the lower leg, called "feathering), had a thicker skin, were less apt to flee and more inclined to stand their ground and fight, and were less sensitive. Desert or arid pony and horse types had lighter coats, thinner manes and tails, no leg feathering, lighter bones, thinner, narrower torsos, and a flighty, sensitive temperament.

From these basic types were created very old breeds such as the Arabian, the Barb, the large European draft and war horses, the Spanish horse, and the Exmoor pony — and all the rest of the breeds with their specialized purposes, body types, and appearances were created by man after that.

WHY DO HORSES SLEEP STANDING UP?

As horses evolved they grew larger, and it became a disadvantage to have to lie down to sleep. Lying down made them vulnerable to predation because it was more difficult to rise and flee quickly. Horses with a special "stay apparatus" in their legs (the first was Dinohippus about five million years ago) were favored by natural selection because they could lock their legs in a standing position and doze upright. This unique equine trait was passed on through the generations of horses.

When a horse locks one hind stifle, the other legs can drop at the hip and rest. Horses sleep a total of five or so hours a day — thirty minutes of which they need to be lying flat on one side to achieve deep REM (rapid eye movement) sleep. When horses are in REM sleep, they peacefully dream, twitch, grunt, and snore.

WHY DO MARES ALWAYS SEEM TO GIVE BIRTH WHEN NO ONE IS LOOKING?

Mares have the ability to delay their foaling until nighttime when everyone else is asleep. Perhaps this is when they feel most relaxed, but in wild conditions, a mare giving birth is at her most vulnerable — not to mention the foal — if there is any sort of predator around. However, despite "safety in numbers," both wild and domestic mares leave the herd and go off alone to give birth.

Mares are most relaxed in a big, clean stall they are familiar with, or on a patch of grass outside (which has been "sterilized" by the sunshine). Mares and their foals need human intervention only if there are complications, but most owners like to be present just in case, and to perform routine medical care for both mother and baby. Normal delivery is a short, explosive process taking about twenty minutes after the water breaks. Most foals are born feet and head first, with one leg preceding the other so the shoulders come out at a narrow slant.

Some people who "imprint train" foals right after they are born feel this is the "golden window of opportunity" for acceptance of humans, so they like to know exactly when the equine stork arrives. Many large breeding barn owners have installed video cameras in their foaling stalls and sensory devices on their mares so that they will know exactly when their mares are giving birth. (You can even watch "foal cams" on the internet!)

WHY DO SOME HORSES "CHANGE" AFTER YOU BUY THEM AND BRING THEM HOME?

Aside from dishonest practices such as sedating a horse to make it seem calmer, or administering a pain blocker to mask lameness, a horse coming to a new home after being sold can go through some normal emotional and physical changes. The stress of leaving one familiar place and ending up in a strange one can cause horses to go off feed and water (beginning with the initial trailer ride). Because horses are so aware of and dependent on a herd or geographical area, they will feel a bit lost until they can rejoin another herd, or bond with you, their new owner. Differences in feed, water, and routine may be hard on some horses emotionally, and physically they need to build up necessary new bacteria in their guts to digest new things, so there may also be tummy aches at first.

If the new rider is at a lower (or higher) level than the previous owner, or gives different cues, the horse may also "test" to see what the new rules are under saddle.

The most positive scenario when a horse is brought to a new home is an improvement in health and well being, especially if the horse was rescued from a bad situation. A horse such as this, however, may give an owner more to deal with than first expected as the horse grows from being weak and sickly to sound and strong.

Why are some horses hard to catch?

Domestic horses can be hard to catch for one major reason — if they associate being haltered and ridden with unpleasantness compared to grazing, playing, resting, or being left alone, then they will try to

avoid the experience. This is the human's fault for the most part. Some owners don't think about the experience from the horse's perspective and roughly handle the bit, jerk up on the girth, or ride their horse too hard. Similar to the problems horses have with trailering, if we make the whole process of catching and riding more enjoyable for the horse, they will stand still and wait for you to halter them — they may even come when you call!

The way to a horse's heart is usually through its stomach, so reward cooperation immediately (but don't bribe them; it doesn't work). If a horse allows you to halter him without running away, let him graze for a few more minutes before leading him away. Make the horse associate haltering with eating — a pleasant thing. Before bridling, warm up the bit in your hands. When tightening the girth, do it slowly and in stages, allowing the horse to relax and move around a bit between each tightening pull.

When riding, don't follow the same old routine until the horse's eyes glaze over and he starts falling asleep. Vary your route and include fun activities. Get off and let your horse graze during a long trail ride. Horses have good memories!

In the case of a horse who is untrained or one that can successfully evade you, make him move away even faster from *you*, but *away* from the other horses and feed until he decides on his own to stand still when you approach. Reward that! If this cannot be done in a large pasture, work on it in a small pen.

WHY DO SOME HORSES EAT DIRT?

Horses seek out mineral-rich riverbanks or areas on the ground to lick if the feed they eat is lacking in iron, phosphorus, calcium, iodine, copper, manganese, or salt. We should give our domestic horses a mineralized salt block not the white variety, which are pure salt, but the red kind) in addition to their hay to make sure they don't resort to licking the dirt, which certainly can cause intestinal problems if they pick up too much sand. Another good supplement is called "free minerals" and comes in a loose form. Horses have been known to eat this source like candy!

Horses eat their own or other horses' dry manure if they are hungry enough. They usually avoid fresh manure, however, and often will not eat grass sprouting from deep, rotting piles of manure. Horses rely on their sense of smell to tell them if food is not fresh, and will normally refuse anything with bacteria, mold, or dirt on it.

Foals will eat their mother's manure, which some say gives them the taste and smell of which plants to graze on before they try grazing on their own, or it is surmised the mother's manure supplies the foal with the necessary gut flora to begin digesting plants.

WHY DO SOME HORSES GO BLIND?

Blindness from injury or disease is common in horses due to the placement and large size of the equine eye. Laceration or infection to any of the parts and layers of the eyeball can cause edema, scarring, cataracts, cysts, or changes that cloud the transparency of the tissue so light

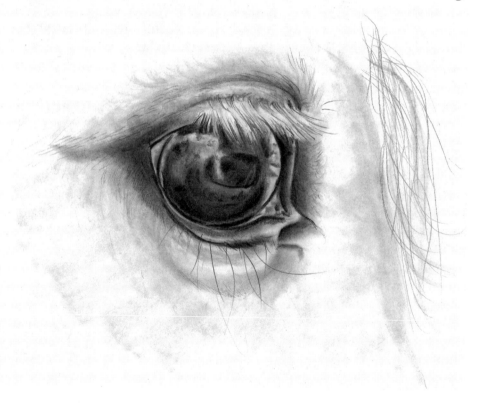

cannot pass through it to the retina. Horses who sustain damage to the optic nerve through head trauma can also lose their eyesight even if their eyes are unharmed.

Because there are no blood vessels in the prominent outer part of the eye (the cornea), helpful blood cells needed to fight eye infection or injury cannot reach these parts until blood vessels have time to grow from nearby tissues. Glaucoma occurs when the clear fluid in the eye either becomes too plentiful or ceases to be produced. Uveitis (inflammation of the parts of the eyes with blood vessels, such as the iris) causes scarring and restriction of movement. Uveitis is commonly known as "moon blindness" because it recurs with a pattern people once thought was related to the moon phases. Uveitis is caused by trauma, parasites, bacteria, fungi, and yeast infection.

If treatment for injury or disease fails and an eye is useless or causing pain, the eye is often removed. The good news is that one-eyed horses can lead useful and happy lives, adjusting quite well if the other eye is functional. Completely blind horses can also remember by smell or touch an area or pathway, and navigate well when all things remain the same, or they can follow a companion animal around. Some horses, like people, are near-sighted, but as of yet there are no eyeglasses made for horses!

WHY DO OLD HORSES HAVE SWAYBACKS?

An old horse can be identified easily by the dip in its back where the saddle sat, and if well-nourished, by the corresponding "haybelly" that protrudes from underneath, which is caused by a slowdown in digestion with age. Horses having long backs and long loins have the greatest problem with swayback, sometimes even at younger ages. The back ligaments of horses can weaken with overuse, carrying many foals, or lack of proper conditioning. When being ridden, swaybacked horses cannot achieve proper collection and their backs get sore. Then they stiffen their necks upward and "hollow" their backs downward away from the pain, which makes the problem worse.

Old horses that are still sound can enjoy the attention, exercise and stimulation of being ridden with a saddle that fits their new contours, and the lightest of riders (such as children). When encouraged to lift and round their backs under these conditions, horses having a swayback condition can also strengthen their back ligaments.

WHY DO TODAY'S HORSES WEAR MASKS, EAR NETS, BLANKETS, SHEETS, AND PAJAMAS?

People who do not own horses often wonder why horses they see in pastures or barns wear strange little hoods over their eyes and noses. "Is your horse blind?" they will ask. "No," you answer, "That is his flymask." If you try a flymask on, you will discover the fine, see-through mesh is the perfect protection from insects, dust, and harmful rays of the sun for the horse's eyes and sometimes the complete nose bridge. Flymasks are especially helpful to pink-skinned horses with a lot of white on their faces who are prone to sunburn and skin and eye cancer. Young, playful horses like to remove each other's flymasks as often as you

put them on — the loud *riiiip* of Velcro seems to satisfy them.

Humans also dress their horses in many types of blankets — especially if the horse's hair has been clipped so the horse doesn't stay as sweaty after being ridden. Lightweight fly or rainsheets protect from the sun, insects, and dampness.

Ear nets are little contraptions that prevent gnats and other insects from gathering in a horse's ear and causing irritation, or sometimes combined with cottonballs in the ear canal, the nets can act as a noise barrier during competition or parades.

If you go to a horse show and

walk through the barns where people are primping their horses, you will be amazed at the things horses are wearing these days. The purpose of all this gear is to keep the horse's body, mane, and tail as neat, clean, and pretty as possible, so when combined with flawless riding, you will place in the ribbons every time.

WHY DO HORSES WEAR BITS IN THEIR MOUTHS?

The bit is a mouthpiece, usually made of metal, that is placed over a horse's tongue in the natural gap (called the "bars") of a horse's jaw between its front and rear teeth, and held in place by a "headstall." There are many variations of headstalls, but generally they contain straps of leather connected to the corners of the bit that encircle the nose and forehead, go around the back of the ears (the poll), under the chin, and around the jaw. However, a headstall does not have to include a bit at all, so how does this work?

A well-trained horse will "give" or flex its head and nose down and inward toward its chest, forming a nice arc with its neck when pressure (not pain) is applied to the bridge of its nose, its poll, or its mouth. A horse in pain will jerk its head up, hollow its back, and open its mouth — such as when heavy hands yank too hard on the sensitive nose bridge, tongue, palette, lips, or flesh under the chin. The reason many people use a bit in a horse's mouth is because they are under the mistaken idea it is the only way they can make a horse stop.

The bit is there for direction and pressure, not for punishment. Any sort of bit with shanks will exert a great deal of pressure, so they need to be used in experienced, light hands. A well-trained horse also feels for the corresponding change in the way a person sits or uses their legs to request a change of gait. It is very possible to ride a horse without the use of a saddle or a bridle when a horse is responsive and well trained.

WHY DO MOST PEOPLE UNIVERSALLY LOVE HORSES SO MUCH?

There is a saying that goes: *The outside of a horse is good for the inside of a man.*

The sight of a horse peacefully grazing in a field can make many people think of kindness, softness, and safety — and for those of us who ride, we are immediately reminded of being powerfully transported far above the ground on a strong, gentle back. We are awed by the athletic power, beauty, and grace of horses, and entertained by their costumed riders. We are fascinated by stories of legendary equines who survived hardship or performed heroic feats, by those who touched their owners deeply or made them proud (and occasionally rich). Some of us are reminded of the "old days" before the combustion engine when horses were an indispensible part of our livelihoods and our lives.

Most of us have never encountered a "rogue" or vicious horse. The bucking broncos at the rodeo are for entertainment, far removed from lesson or camp horses we have loved and learned from, trail or dude ranch mounts we have rented and enjoyed on our vacations. We are continually amazed when meeting horses that despite their size and power, they are affectionate and sweet, and grateful for their feed and care.

There will always be a part of us that needs to be with other animals, and the horse is unequalled as a closely-knit partner capable of carrying us away for fun and adventure.

LISA DINES

is also the author of

THE AMERICAN MUSTANG GUIDEBOOK
History, Behavior, and State-by-State Directions on
Where to Best View America's Wild Horses

also published by Willow Creek Press

BETH MESSINA

is a graphic designer and illustrator whose
award-winning work can be found in collections
internationally as well as across the United States.
Her primary media is graphite, and her
primary subject is horses.